MW01291475

EASY

COOKBOOK

THE EFFORTLESS CHEF SERIES

VOL. #XXXVIII

By
Chef Maggie Chow

Copyright © 2015 by Saxonberg
Associates
All rights reserved

Published by
BookSumo, a division of Saxonberg
Associates
http://www.booksumo.com/

A GIFT FROM ME TO YOU...

Send the Book!

I know you like easy cooking. But what about Japanese Sushi?

Join my private reader's club and get a copy of ***Infinite Sushi: A Complete Set of Sushi and Japanese Recipes*** by fellow BookSumo author Hashimoto Kazuma for FREE!

Send the Book!

Enjoy some of the best sushi available!

You will also receive updates about all my new books when they are free. So please show your support.

Also don't forget to like and subscribe on the social networks. I love meeting my readers. Links to all my profiles are below so please click and connect :)

Facebook

Twitter

ABOUT THE AUTHOR.

Maggie Chow is the author and creator of your favorite *Easy Cookbooks* and *The Effortless Chef Series*. Maggie is a lover of all things related to food. Maggie loves nothing more than finding new recipes, trying them out, and then making them her own, by adding or removing ingredients, tweaking cooking times, and anything to make the recipe not only taste better, but be easier to cook!

For a complete listing of all my books please see my author page.

INTRODUCTION

Welcome to *The Effortless Chef Series*! Thank you for taking the time to download the *Easy Pasta Cookbook*. Come take a journey with me into the delights of easy cooking. The point of this cookbook and all my cookbooks is to exemplify the effortless nature of cooking simply.

In this book we focus on Pasta. You will find that even though the recipes are simple, the taste of the dishes is quite amazing.

So will you join me in an adventure of simple cooking? If the answer is yes (and I hope it is) please consult the table of contents to find the dishes you are most interested in. Once you are ready jump right in and start cooking.

— Chef Maggie Chow

TABLE OF CONTENTS

ANY ISSUES? CONTACT ME

If you find that something important to you is missing from this book please contact me at maggie@booksumo.com.

I will try my best to re-publish a revised copy taking your feedback into consideration and let you know when the book has been revised with you in mind.

:)

— Chef Maggie Chow

NOTICE TO PRINT READERS:

Hey, because you purchased the print version of this book you are entitled to its original digital version for free by Amazon.

So when you have the time, please review your purchases, and download the Kindle version of this book.

You might enjoy consuming this book more in its original digital format.

;)

But, in any case, take care and enjoy reading in whatever format you choose!

LEGAL NOTES

ALL RIGHTS RESERVED. NO PART OF THIS BOOK MAY BE REPRODUCED OR TRANSMITTED IN ANY FORM OR BY ANY MEANS. PHOTOCOPYING, POSTING ONLINE, AND / OR DIGITAL COPYING IS STRICTLY PROHIBITED UNLESS WRITTEN PERMISSION IS GRANTED BY THE BOOK'S PUBLISHING COMPANY. LIMITED USE OF THE BOOK'S TEXT IS PERMITTED FOR USE IN REVIEWS WRITTEN FOR THE PUBLIC AND/OR PUBLIC DOMAIN.

COMMON ABBREVIATIONS

cup(s)	C.
tablespoon	tbsp
teaspoon	tsp
ounce	oz
pound	lb

CHAPTER 1: EASY PASTA RECIPES

TOMATO PARMESAN SPINACH

Ingredients

- 3/4 lb pasta
- 1 tbsp olive oil
- 1 lb spicy Italian sausage
- 1 onion, chopped
- 4 cloves garlic, diced
- 1 (14.5 oz) can chicken broth
- 1 tsp dried basil
- 1 (14.5 oz) can diced tomatoes
- 1 (10 oz) package frozen chopped spinach
- 1/2 C. grated Parmesan cheese

Directions

- For 8 mins boil pasta in water and salt until al dente. Remove excess water.
- Get a frying pan. Stir fry your garlic and onions in oil. Then for 5 mins fry your sausage until fully cooked. Mix in your basil, tomatoes (with sauce), and broth.
- Add your spinach then lightly boil for 6 mins or spinach becomes soft.
- Combine pasta and sausage cook for 2 mins. Then garnish with cheese.
- Enjoy.

Servings: 6 servings

Timing Information:

Preparation	Cooking	Total Time
15 mins	30 mins	45 mins

Nutritional Information:

Calories	423 kcal
Carbohydrates	39 g
Cholesterol	89 mg
Fat	19.3 g
Fiber	4.5 g
Protein	22.3 g
Sodium	1077 mg

* Percent Daily Values are based on a 2,000 calorie diet.

PASTA TOMATO SOUP

Ingredients

- 1 tbsp olive oil
- 2 stalks celery, chopped
- 1 onion, chopped
- 3 cloves garlic, diced
- 2 tsps dried parsley
- 1 tsp Italian seasoning
- 1/4 tsp mashed red pepper flakes
- salt to taste
- 1 (14.5 oz) can chicken broth
- 2 medium tomatoes, peeled and chopped
- 1 (8 oz) can tomato sauce
- 1/2 C. uncooked spinach pasta
- 1 (15 oz) can cannellini beans, with liquid

Directions

- Stir fry your salt, celery, red pepper flakes, onions, Italian seasoning, parsley, and garlic in olive oil for 6 mins.

- Combine in tomato sauce, broth, and tomatoes. Bring everything to a light boil over medium to low heat and cook for 17 mins.
- Mix in your pasta and continue cooking for 12 more mins until pasta is soft.
- Finally combine in your beans with sauce, and heat them up. Garnish everything with some parmesan.
- Enjoy.

Servings: 4 servings

Timing Information:

Preparation	Cooking	Total Time
10 mins	40 mins	50 mins

Nutritional Information:

Calories	225 kcal
Carbohydrates	37.3 g
Cholesterol	2 mg
Fat	4.4 g
Fiber	7.9 g
Protein	11 g
Sodium	758 mg

* Percent Daily Values are based on a 2,000 calorie diet.

Pasta Mediterraneo

Ingredients

- 1 (8 oz) package linguine pasta
- 3 slices bacon
- 1 lb boneless chicken breast half, cooked and diced
- salt to taste
- 1 (14.5 oz) can peeled and diced tomatoes with juice
- 1/4 tsp dried rosemary
- 1/3 C. crumbled feta cheese
- 2/3 C. pitted black olives
- 1 (6 oz) can artichoke hearts, drained

Directions

- For 10 mins boil pasta in salt and water.
- Get a frying pan: fry your bacon and then break it into pieces and place it to the side.

- Re-heat your frying pan and simmer the following for 20 mins: tomatoes, chicken, salt, bacon, and rosemary.
- Add your olives, feta, and artichokes, and heat them.
- Finally add in your pasta and r evenly.
- Garnish with more cheese if you like.
- Enjoy.

Servings: 4 servings

Timing Information:

Preparation	Cooking	Total Time
15 mins	20 mins	40 mins

Nutritional Information:

Calories	625 kcal
Carbohydrates	50.8 g
Cholesterol	111 mg
Fat	26.6 g
Fiber	5 g
Protein	45.3 g
Sodium	911 mg

* Percent Daily Values are based on a 2,000 calorie diet.

Quick Mozzarella Pasta Salad

Ingredients

- 1 (8 oz) package farfalle (bow tie) pasta
- 20 cherry tomatoes, halved
- 7 oz bocconcini (fresh mozzarella)
- 3/4 C. black olives
- 2 tbsps olive oil
- 6 fresh basil leaves
- 1 1/2 tsps fresh oregano leaves

Directions

- Boil your bow tie pasta for 12 mins in salt and water. Then drain excess liquid. Let it set to room temp.
- Get a bowl and mix: oregano, tomatoes, basil, olives, bocconcini, olive oil, and pasta.
- Enjoy at room temp. or chilled.

Servings: 4 servings

Timing Information:

Preparation	Cooking	Total Time
15 mins	15 mins	45 mins

Nutritional Information:

Calories	451 kcal
Carbohydrates	47.6 g
Cholesterol	39 mg
Fat	21.8 g
Fiber	3.7 g
Protein	17.3 g
Sodium	314 mg

* Percent Daily Values are based on a 2,000 calorie diet.

Tortellini Spinach Soup

Ingredients

- 1 1/2 tbsps olive oil
- 1 tsp tomato paste
- 1 anchovy fillet, chopped
- 4 C. chicken broth
- 1 C. dry cheese tortellini
- 1 (15 oz) can white beans, rinsed and drained
- salt and ground black pepper to taste
- 1 pinch red pepper flakes
- 1 pinch dried oregano
- 2 C. baby spinach leaves
- 1/4 C. grated Parmesan cheese
- 1 pinch red pepper flakes, or to taste

Directions

- Get a saucepan, with oil, cook for 3 mins: anchovy, and tomato paste.
- Add your broth and heat it until boiling, then add beans and noodles. Boil for 10 mins. Then lower heat to a light simmer.
- Finally add oregano, salt, red pepper flakes, spinach, and black pepper, and simmer for 5 mins.
- Garnish with parmesan and enjoy.

Servings: 4 servings

Timing Information:

Preparation	Cooking	Total Time
10 mins	20 mins	30 mins

Nutritional Information:

Calories	293 kcal
Carbohydrates	35.9 g
Cholesterol	24 mg
Fat	10.1 g
Fiber	6.7 g
Protein	15.4 g
Sodium	1256 mg

* Percent Daily Values are based on a 2,000 calorie diet.

THE BEST MACARONI SALAD

Ingredients

Dressing:

- 1/4 C. mayonnaise
- 1/4 C. sour cream
- 1/4 C. crumbled blue cheese
- 1 1/2 tsps milk
- 1/2 tsp honey mustard
- 1/2 tsp white vinegar
- 1/2 tsp salt
- 1/4 tsp garlic powder
- 1/4 tsp ground black pepper
- 1/8 tsp cayenne pepper

Salad:

- 2 1/2 C. penne pasta
- 2 tbsps olive oil
- 1 clove garlic, diced
- 3/4 tsp diced fresh basil
- 2 1/2 C. cauliflower florets
- 2 C. halved cherry tomatoes
- 1/2 C. chopped red bell pepper

- 4 oz mozzarella cheese, cut into 1-inch strips
- 3 green onions, chopped
- 2 tbsps grated Parmesan cheese

Directions

- Get a bowl, mix evenly: cayenne, mayo, black pepper, sour cream, garlic powder, blue cheese, salt, milk, vinegar, and honey mustard.
- For 12 mins boil your noodles in salt and water. Then remove excess water, and set aside.
- Fry your garlic and basil in olive oil for 4 mins. And use as a coating for your pasta.
- Combine with your pasta: parmesan, cauliflower, green onion, tomatoes, mozzarella, and red bell peppers.
- Chill in the frig for 1 hr.
- Enjoy.

Servings: 12 servings

Timing Information:

Preparation	Cooking	Total Time
30 mins	15 mins	1 hr 45 mins

Nutritional Information:

Calories	285 kcal
Carbohydrates	38.3 g
Cholesterol	13 mg
Fat	10.7 g
Fiber	2.7 g
Protein	10.5 g
Sodium	250 mg

* Percent Daily Values are based on a 2,000 calorie diet.

RESTAURANT STYLE LINGUINE

Ingredients

- 2 (8 oz) packages fresh linguine pasta
- 1 C. cream
- 4 oz smoked salmon, chopped
- 1 pinch freshly grated nutmeg (optional)
- 1 pinch ground black pepper, or to taste (optional)
- 1 1/2 tbsps black caviar
- 1 bunch chopped flat leaf parsley

Directions

- Boil your pasta in water and salt for 7 to 10 mins until al dente. Drain the liquid and set aside.
- Get a saucepan and heat up your cream, then cook your salmon with pepper and nutmeg. Coat

the pasta with this mixture. Add
caviar as well.

- Garnish everything with some
parsley.
- Enjoy.

Servings: 4 servings

Timing Information:

Preparation	Cooking	Total Time
10 mins	10 mins	20 mins

Nutritional Information:

Calories	583 kcal
Carbohydrates	64.4 g
Cholesterol	205 mg
Fat	27.1 g
Fiber	5 g
Protein	21 g
Sodium	373 mg

* Percent Daily Values are based on a 2,000 calorie diet.

MAGGIE'S FAVORITE EASY RIGATONI

Ingredients

- 1/4 C. olive oil
- 2 cloves garlic, diced
- 1 eggplant, peeled and cut into 1/2-inch cubes
- 1 (28 oz) can plum tomatoes with juice, chopped
- 1 (16 oz) package rigatoni pasta

Directions

- Boil your rigatoni in salt and water for 12 mins until al dente. Remove excess liquid and set aside.
- Get a frying pan: stir fry your garlic for 3 mins in olive oil. Add in your eggplants and fry for another 6 mins. Combine in your

tomatoes and juice and simmer
for 22 mins.
- Cover pasta with eggplants and
sauce.
- Enjoy.

Servings: 8 servings

Timing Information:

Preparation	Cooking	Total Time
15 mins	40 mins	55 mins

Nutritional Information:

Calories	295 kcal
Carbohydrates	48.8 g
Cholesterol	0 mg
Fat	8.3 g
Fiber	5.2 g
Protein	8.9 g
Sodium	145 mg

* Percent Daily Values are based on a 2,000 calorie diet.

CREAMY CHICKEN FETTUCCINE

Ingredients

- 1 lb dry fettuccine pasta
- 2 tbsps vegetable oil
- 1/4 C. sliced onions
- 1/2 C. chopped yellow squash
- 1/2 C. zucchini, cut diagonally into 1/2 inch thick slices
- 3/4 C. sliced mushrooms (optional)
- 1 1/4 C. heavy cream
- 1 jalapeno pepper, seeded and diced
- 1 tsp diced garlic
- 1 tbsp Dijon mustard
- 1 tbsp Cajun seasoning
- 1/2 C. grated Parmesan cheese
- 1/2 C. diced tomatoes
- salt and pepper to taste
- 3 tbsps vegetable oil
- 1 lb chicken breast, cut into 1/2 inch pieces
- flour for dredging

Directions

- Boil your fettuccine for 10 mins in water and salt.
- Get a frying pan, heat some oil, and stir fry for 5 mins: mushrooms, onions, zucchini, and squash.
- Combine with the onions your cream and pasta and lightly simmer for 5 mins. Now add cajun seasoning, jalapeno, mustard, and garlic. Simmer for 2 more mins.
- Get a 2nd pan and cook your chicken after it has been coated with flour in 3 tbsps of oil until completely done.
- Combine everything together, chicken, veggies, and pasta.
- Enjoy.

Servings: 6 servings

Timing Information:

Preparation	Cooking	Total Time
20 mins	25 mins	45 mins

Nutritional Information:

Calories	807 kcal
Carbohydrates	69.1 g
Cholesterol	74 mg
Fat	36.8 g
Fiber	4.1 g
Protein	50.2 g
Sodium	605 mg

* Percent Daily Values are based on a 2,000 calorie diet.

QUICK STOVETOP PASTA

Ingredients

- 1 (8 oz) package campanelle (little bells) pasta
- 1/2 C. ricotta cheese
- 2 tbsps olive oil
- 1/4 onion, chopped
- 1 (6.5 oz) can tomato sauce

Directions

- Boil pasta in salt and water for 13 mins. Drain liquid and place in a bowl with ricotta, mix everything evenly.
- Get a frying pan and fry onions in olive oil for 8 mins. Combine in your: tomato sauce. Stir fry for 4 mins.
- Cover your noodles with the sauce, and let it sit for 7 mins.
- Enjoy.

Servings: 4 servings

Timing Information:

Preparation	Cooking	Total Time
10 mins	20 mins	30 mins

Nutritional Information:

Calories	328 kcal
Carbohydrates	47.4 g
Cholesterol	10 mg
Fat	10.2 g
Fiber	2.7 g
Protein	11.7 g
Sodium	284 mg

* Percent Daily Values are based on a 2,000 calorie diet.

SHRIMP PENNE

Ingredients

- 6 oz penne pasta
- 1 onion, chopped
- 2 tbsps olive oil
- 1 clove garlic, diced
- 1 green bell pepper, sliced
- 3 stalks celery, chopped
- 1 (14.5 oz) can diced tomatoes
- 1 1/2 C. dry hard cider
- 1 1/2 tbsps tomato paste
- salt to taste
- ground black pepper to taste
- 3/4 lb fresh prawns

Directions

- Fry your onions for 4 mins in olive oil. Then add the following: celery, garlic, and bell pepper. Fry for 6 more mins.

- Combine with the onions: salt, tomatoes, pepper, tomato puree, and dry cider. Get it boiling.
- Once boiling combine in your pasta. Place a lid on the pan. Lightly boil for 20 mins.
- Add your prawns to everything and continue simmering for 6 more mins.
- Enjoy.

Servings: 4 servings

Timing Information:

Preparation	Cooking	Total Time
10 mins	30 mins	40 mins

Nutritional Information:

Calories	411 kcal
Carbohydrates	50.4 g
Cholesterol	0 mg
Fat	9.3 g
Fiber	3.8 g
Protein	24 g
Sodium	313 mg

* Percent Daily Values are based on a 2,000 calorie diet.

CANNELLINI CLASSIC

Ingredients

- 3 cloves garlic, diced
- 1 onion, chopped
- 1 carrot, finely chopped
- 2 tbsps chopped fresh parsley
- 2 tsps dried basil
- 1 tsp dried oregano
- 4 tbsps olive oil
- 1 (14.5 oz) can whole peeled tomatoes
- 2 C. cooked cannellini beans, drained and rinsed
- 8 oz macaroni
- 2 tbsps butter
- 1/4 C. grated Parmesan cheese
- salt and pepper to taste

Directions

- Stir fry, in olive oil, until onions are soft: onions, basil, carrots, garlic, parsley, and oregano. Mix in some salt and pepper, tomatoes, and 1/4 C. of tomato juice. Cook for 12 mins.

- Combine in the cannellini and place a lid on the pan. Simmer for 20 mins with lower heat.
- Boil your macaroni in salt and water until al dente about 10 to 12 mins. Then coat with butter and parmesan. Mix the coated noodles with the cannellini and enjoy.

Servings: 4 to 6 servings

Timing Information:

Preparation	Cooking	Total Time
10 mins	40 mins	50 mins

Nutritional Information:

Calories	452 kcal
Carbohydrates	59.3 g
Cholesterol	16 mg
Fat	17.7 g
Fiber	7.9 g
Protein	15.7 g
Sodium	228 mg

* Percent Daily Values are based on a 2,000 calorie diet.

PECOS PASTA

Ingredients

- 4 oz macaroni
- 1 tbsp butter
- 1 green bell pepper, chopped
- 1 onion, chopped
- 1 (8.75 oz) can whole kernel corn, drained
- 1 (15 oz) can chili with beans
- 1 tsp salt
- 1 tsp ground black pepper

Directions

- Boil your macaroni in salt and water for 10 mins. Remove liquid excesses.
- Fry your, diced onions, and diced bell pepper in butter until onion is soft. Mix in some salt and pepper, chili beans, and corn.

Lower your heating source and let everything simmer for 6 mins.
- Finally combine in your macaroni and place a lid on the pan. Simmer for another 5 mins.
- Enjoy.

Servings: 4 servings

Timing Information:

Preparation	Cooking	Total Time
10 mins	20 mins	30 mins

Nutritional Information:

Calories	315 kcal
Carbohydrates	49.2 g
Cholesterol	25 mg
Fat	9.7 g
Fiber	7.8 g
Protein	11.9 g
Sodium	1336 mg

* Percent Daily Values are based on a 2,000 calorie diet.

THE BEST PESTO

Ingredients

- 4 C. packed fresh basil leaves
- 1/4 C. Italian parsley
- 2 cloves garlic, peeled and lightly mashed
- 1 C. pine nuts
- 1 1/2 C. shredded Parmigiano-Reggiano cheese
- 1 tbsp fresh lemon juice
- 1/2 C. extra-virgin olive oil, or more as needed
- salt and ground black pepper to taste

Directions

- For 1 min, pulse the following in the food processor: garlic, basil, parsley, parmesan, and pine nuts.
- Finally keep the machine running and add olive oil, and lemon

juice. Continue processing until completely smooth. Add your preferred about of pepper and salt.

- Enjoy.

NOTE: Use over angel hair cooked until al dente.

Servings: 6 servings

Timing Information:

Preparation	Cooking	Total Time
15 mins		15 mins

Nutritional Information:

Calories	389 kcal
Carbohydrates	5.4 g
Cholesterol	14 mg
Fat	35.8 g
Fiber	1.6 g
Protein	14.1 g
Sodium	343 mg

* Percent Daily Values are based on a 2,000 calorie diet.

COUNTRYSIDE FUSILI AND PEPPERS

Ingredients

- 1 lb rotini or fusili pasta
- 6 slices bacon
- 1/2 C. extra virgin olive oil
- 2 medium onions, chopped
- 1 red bell pepper, chopped
- 1/4 C. chopped parsley
- 4 cloves garlic, diced
- Salt (optional)
- 1/2 tsp mashed red pepper flakes
- 1 (28 oz) can plum tomatoes, undrained, chopped
- 1/2 C. Pitted Olives
- 2 tbsps capers, drained
- 1/2 tsp dried oregano
- 1/2 C. grated Parmesan cheese

Directions

- Boil pasta for 10 mins in salted water. Remove liquid and set aside in a bowl.
- Get a frying pan and fry bacon until cooked. Set aside. Remove bacon oil and add new oil.
- Stir fry your onions for 6 mins. Then combine in some pepper flakes, bell pepper, garlic, and parsley. Stir fry for 3 more mins. Combine in your bacon and tomatoes, and let the contents lightly boil for 10 mins.
- Finally mix in oregano, and olive. Cook for another 3 mins. Add your preferred amount of salt.
- Add sauce to the pasta with cheese, and mix everything nicely.
- Enjoy.

Servings: 6 servings

Timing Information:

Preparation	Cooking	Total Time
25 mins	25 mins	50 mins

Nutritional Information:

Calories	593 kcal
Carbohydrates	68.6 g
Cholesterol	16 mg
Fat	27.6 g
Fiber	5.1 g
Protein	17.8 g
Sodium	770 mg

* Percent Daily Values are based on a 2,000 calorie diet.

PASTA RUSTIC

Ingredients

- 1 lb farfalle (bow tie) pasta
- 1/3 C. olive oil
- 1 clove garlic, chopped
- 1/4 C. butter
- 2 small zucchini, quartered and sliced
- 1 onion, chopped
- 1 tomato, chopped
- 1 (8 oz) package mushrooms, sliced
- 1 tbsp dried oregano
- 1 tbsp paprika
- salt and pepper to taste

Directions

- Boil your pasta for 10 mins in water and salt. Remove excess liquid and set aside.

- Fry your salt, pepper, garlic, paprika, zucchini, oregano, mushrooms, onion, and tomato, for 17 mins in olive oil.
- Mix the veggies and pasta.
- Enjoy.

Servings: 4 servings

Timing Information:

Preparation	Cooking	Total Time
10 mins	25 mins	35 mins

Nutritional Information:

Calories	717 kcal
Carbohydrates	92.8 g
Cholesterol	31 mg
Fat	32.9 g
Fiber	7.5 g
Protein	18.1 g
Sodium	491 mg

* Percent Daily Values are based on a 2,000 calorie diet.

Simple Sundried Tomato Pasta

Ingredients

- 2/3 C. chopped fresh basil
- 1 (28 oz) can diced tomatoes
- 1 1/2 tsps diced garlic
- 1 (6 oz) can sliced black olives
- 1 1/2 C. olive oil
- 1 tsp salt
- 1 tsp ground black pepper
- 1/2 C. chopped fresh chives
- 1/2 C. chopped sun-dried tomatoes
- 1 tsp mashed red pepper flakes
- 6 oz goat cheese
- 2 (16 oz) packages farfalle pasta

Directions

- Get a bowl, mix: pepper flakes, basil, sun dried tomatoes, diced tomatoes, chives, garlic, pepper, olives, salt, and olive oil. Place plastic over the bowl, and set in the frig for 7 to 12 hours.

- Before using the mix, let it get to room temp.
- Boil your pasta in salt and water for 10 mins. Remove the excess liquid, mix pasta with sauce, and goat cheese.
- Enjoy.

Servings: 6 to 8 servings

Timing Information:

Preparation	Cooking	Total Time
8 hrs	20 mins	8 hrs 20 mins

Nutritional Information:

Calories	1027 kcal
Carbohydrates	102.5 g
Cholesterol	19 mg
Fat	59.4 g
Fiber	6.9 g
Protein	24.5 g
Sodium	857 mg

* Percent Daily Values are based on a 2,000 calorie diet.

PEPPERONI PASTA

Ingredients

- 2 tbsps olive oil
- 1 clove garlic, mashed
- 1 onion, diced
- 1 large tomato, cubed
- 1 C. kalamata olives, pitted and chopped
- 1/3 C. sliced pepperoni sausage, cut into strips
- 1/2 C. sliced fresh mushrooms
- 2 tbsps capers
- salt and pepper to taste
- 1 lb pasta
- 1 C. smoked mozzarella cheese, cubed

Directions

- Boil your pasta for 10 mins in water and salt. Then drain the water. Set aside.

- Get a frying pan, stir fry: onions, and garlic, in olive oil until onions are see through.
- Combine in your salt and pepper, tomato, pepperoni, capers, olives, and mushrooms. Bring to a simmer for 3 mins.
- Finally add your pasta to the sauce. Garnish with mozzarella.
- Enjoy.

Servings: 6 servings

Timing Information:

Preparation	Cooking	Total Time
20 mins	20 mins	40 mins

Nutritional Information:

Calories	517 kcal
Carbohydrates	62.3 g
Cholesterol	28 mg
Fat	21.4 g
Fiber	3.5 g
Protein	18 g
Sodium	782 mg

* Percent Daily Values are based on a 2,000 calorie diet.

A LIGHT THAI INSPIRED PASTA

Ingredients

- 1 tbsp sesame oil
- 8 oz dry fettuccine pasta
- 1/2 tsp soy sauce
- 2 green onions, chopped
- 3/4 C. fresh bean sprouts
- 1 pinch cayenne pepper
- 1 pinch ground white pepper
- 1 pinch garlic powder
- 1 tbsp toasted sesame seeds

Directions

- Boil your pasta for 10 mins in salt and water. Drain excess liquid. Set aside.
- Get a frying pan, stir fry: pasta, soy sauce, garlic powder, green onions, pepper, bean sprouts, black pepper, and cayenne for 5 mins.

- Garnish with toasted sesame.
- Enjoy.

Servings: 4 servings

Timing Information:

Preparation	Cooking	Total Time
10 mins	5 mins	15 mins

Nutritional Information:

Calories	254 kcal
Carbohydrates	43.4 g
Cholesterol	0 mg
Fat	5.9 g
Fiber	2.8 g
Protein	8.7 g
Sodium	43 mg

* Percent Daily Values are based on a 2,000 calorie diet.

BACON LINGUINE

Ingredients

- 5 shallots, chopped
- 4 cloves garlic, chopped
- 6 oz pancetta bacon, diced
- 2 C. fresh sliced mushrooms
- 2 pinches freshly ground black pepper
- 2 pinches dried oregano
- 1/2 C. chicken broth
- 1/4 C. olive oil
- 1 (12 oz) package linguine pasta
- 1/2 C. freshly grated Parmesan cheese

Directions

- Boil your pasta for 10 mins in salt and water. Remove excess liquid. Set to the side.
- Get a frying pan and fry your bacon until brown. Then mix in

your mushrooms, shallots, and garlic. Cook for another 2 mins. Finally add your broth, oregano, and pepper.

- Boil everything for 2 mins. Place a lid on the pan. Lower the heat and simmer for 8 mins.
- Cover your pasta with the broth and some olive oil. Garnish the pasta with some more pancetta, mushrooms, and parmesan.
- Enjoy.

Servings: 6 servings

Timing Information:

Preparation	Cooking	Total Time
5 mins	10 mins	15 mins

Nutritional Information:

Calories	477 kcal
Carbohydrates	50.1 g
Cholesterol	25 mg
Fat	25 g
Fiber	2.7 g
Protein	15.2 g
Sodium	345 mg

* Percent Daily Values are based on a 2,000 calorie diet.

Easy Mushroom Pasta

Ingredients

- 1 (16 oz) package egg noodles
- 1 (10.75 oz) can condensed cream of mushroom soup
- 1 C. cubed processed cheese
- 2 tbsps butter
- 1/4 C. milk
- 1 tsp garlic powder
- salt and pepper to taste

Directions

- Boil your pasta in salt and water for 10 mins. Remove excess liquid.
- Get a pan and heat and stir until cheese melted: salt and pepper, mushroom soup, garlic powder, cheese, milk, and butter.

- Once your cheese is melted mix in your noodles and heat for 1 more min. Coat evenly.
- Enjoy.

Servings: 5 servings

Timing Information:

Preparation	Cooking	Total Time
3 mins	12 mins	15 mins

Nutritional Information:

Calories	526 kcal
Carbohydrates	64.2 g
Cholesterol	106 mg
Fat	22 g
Fiber	2.7 g
Protein	18.2 g
Sodium	889 mg

* Percent Daily Values are based on a 2,000 calorie diet.

Cajun Style Penne

Ingredients

- 1 lb penne pasta
- 2 tbsps butter, divided
- 4 boneless, skinless chicken breasts, trimmed of fat and cut crosswise into 1/4-inch slices
- 2 tbsps Cajun-style blackened seasoning
- 4 cloves garlic, chopped
- 1 large red onion, cut into wedges
- 1 green bell pepper, seeded and sliced into strips
- 1 red bell pepper, seeded and sliced into strips
- 1 yellow bell pepper, seeded and sliced into strips
- 1 tsp mashed red pepper flakes
- 1/4 tsp curry powder
- salt and pepper to taste
- 2 (24 oz) jars meatless spaghetti sauce

Directions

- Boil pasta in salt and water for 10 mins. Drain excess liquid. Set aside.
- Get a frying pan and stir fry your chicken in 1 tbsp of butter until fully done and brown. Remove chicken from the pan.
- Fry onions, salt and pepper, garlic, curry powder, all the julienned peppers, and red pepper flakes until the onions have browned and everything is soft. Mix back in your chicken and the tomato sauce.
- Heat for 3 mins. Let the flavors settle for 5 mins.
- Enjoy.

Servings: 8 servings

Timing Information:

Preparation	Cooking	Total Time
15 mins	30 mins	45 mins

Nutritional Information:

Calories	457 kcal
Carbohydrates	68 g
Cholesterol	45 mg
Fat	9.6 g
Fiber	7 g
Protein	24.7 g
Sodium	1107 mg

* Percent Daily Values are based on a 2,000 calorie diet.

Fresh Seasoning Pasta

Ingredients

- 1/2 lb uncooked pasta
- 1/2 C. butter
- 4 cloves garlic, diced
- 3 tbsps chopped fresh basil
- 1 tbsp chopped fresh thyme
- 1 tsp dried marjoram
- 1 tsp ground savory
- 1 tbsp chopped fresh parsley
- salt to taste
- ground black pepper to taste
- 2 tbsps sliced black olives

Directions

- Boil pasta in salt and water for 10 mins. Remove liquid and set aside.
- Get a frying pan and melt some butter, and all the seasonings.

Cook for 3 mins to flavor your butter.

- Coat your pasta with the flavored butter. Add some salt and pepper, and garnish with olives.
- Enjoy.

Servings: 4 servings

Timing Information:

Preparation	Cooking	Total Time
15 mins	15 mins	30 mins

Nutritional Information:

Calories	379 kcal
Carbohydrates	32.9 g
Cholesterol	102 mg
Fat	24.8 g
Fiber	2.8 g
Protein	7.1 g
Sodium	216 mg

* Percent Daily Values are based on a 2,000 calorie diet.

ALFREDO DONE RIGHT

Ingredients

- 6 oz dry fettuccine pasta
- 1 (8 oz) package cream cheese
- 6 tbsps butter
- 1/2 C. milk
- 1/2 tsp garlic powder
- salt and pepper to taste
- 2 skinless, boneless chicken breast halves - cooked and cubed
- 2 C. chopped fresh broccoli
- 2 small zucchini, julienned
- 1/2 C. chopped red bell pepper

Directions

- Boil your pasta in salt and water for 10 mins. Remove excess liquid and set aside.
- Get a frying pan and mix: milk, garlic powder, cream cheese, salt, pepper, and butter. Heat until

cheese is melted and everything is even and smooth. Lightly boil for 4 mins to increase thickness.

- Add your chicken, red pepper, zucchini, and broccoli and continue simmering for 4 more mins.
- Toss pasta with alfredo.
- Enjoy.

Servings: 4 servings

Timing Information:

Preparation	Cooking	Total Time
20 mins	20 mins	40 mins

Nutritional Information:

Calories	645 kcal
Carbohydrates	39.7 g
Cholesterol	151 mg
Fat	42.7 g
Fiber	3.7 g
Protein	28.3 g
Sodium	355 mg

* Percent Daily Values are based on a 2,000 calorie diet.

Pasta Cajun II

Ingredients

- 4 oz linguine pasta
- 2 skinless, boneless chicken breast halves
- 2 tsps Cajun seasoning
- 2 tbsps butter
- 1 red bell pepper, sliced
- 1 green bell pepper, sliced
- 4 fresh mushrooms, sliced
- 1 green onion, chopped
- 1 C. heavy cream
- 1/4 tsp dried basil
- 1/4 tsp lemon pepper
- 1/4 tsp salt
- 1/8 tsp garlic powder
- 1/8 tsp ground black pepper
- 1/4 C. grated Parmesan cheese

Directions

- Boil pasta in salt and water for 10 mins. Remove liquid excess. Set aside.
- Coat your chicken with Cajun seasoning evenly. Then fry in butter for 8 mins. Continue stir frying the chicken with: green onion, mushrooms, and red and green bell peppers for 4 more mins.
- Set the heat to low and combine in your garlic powder, cream, lemon pepper, salt, basil, and black pepper. Heat for 3 mins. Then mix in your pasta and heat for another 2 mins.
- Garnish with some parmesan.
- Enjoy.

Servings: 2 servings

Timing Information:

Preparation	Cooking	Total Time
20 mins	20 mins	40 mins

Nutritional Information:

Calories	935 kcal
Carbohydrates	54 g
Cholesterol	271 mg
Fat	61.7 g
Fiber	5 g
Protein	43.7 g
Sodium	1189 mg

* Percent Daily Values are based on a 2,000 calorie diet.

A GIFT FROM ME TO YOU...

Send the Book!

I know you like easy cooking. But what about Japanese Sushi?

Join my private reader's club and get a copy of *Infinite Sushi: A Complete Set of Sushi and Japanese Recipes* by fellow BookSumo author Hashimoto Kazuma for FREE!

Send the Book!

Enjoy some of the best sushi available!

You will also receive updates about all my new books when they are free. So please show your support.

Also don't forget to like and subscribe on the social networks. I love meeting my readers. Links to all my profiles are below so please click and connect :)

Facebook

Twitter

COME ON...
LET'S BE FRIENDS :)

I adore my readers and love connecting with them socially. Please follow the links below so we can connect on Facebook, Twitter, and Google+.

Facebook

Twitter

I also have a blog that I regularly update for my readers so check it out below.

My Blog

CAN I ASK A FAVOUR?

If you found this book interesting, or have otherwise found any benefit in it. Then may I ask that you post a review of it on Amazon? Nothing excites me more than new reviews, especially reviews which suggest new topics for writing. I do read all reviews and I always factor feedback into my newer works.

So if you are willing to take ten minutes to write what you sincerely thought about this book then please visit our Amazon page and post your opinions.

Again thank you!

INTERESTED IN OTHER EASY COOKBOOKS?

Everything is easy! Check out my Amazon Author page for more great cookbooks:

For a complete listing of all my books please see my author page.

45709016R00053

Made in the USA
Middletown, DE
12 July 2017